0X 7/11 0X ✓4/14
1X 10-14/9-15
RB
S0-CCG-132

Doomsday Scenarios: Separating Fact from Fiction™

CYBERTERRORISM

Jacqueline Ching

3 1336 08693 3018

rosen publishing's
rosen central®

New York

For Scotia and Dagny

Published in 2010 by The Rosen Publishing Group, Inc.
29 East 21st Street, New York, NY 10010

Copyright © 2010 by The Rosen Publishing Group, Inc.

First Edition

All rights reserved. No part of this book may be reproduced in any form without permission in writing from the publisher, except by a reviewer.

Library of Congress Cataloging-in-Publication Data

Ching, Jacqueline.
Cyberterrorism / Jacqueline Ching.
p. cm.—(Doomsday scenarios: separating fact from fiction)
Includes bibliographical references and index.
ISBN 978-1-4358-3565-8 (library binding)
ISBN 978-1-4358-8532-5 (pbk)
ISBN 978-1-4358-8533-2 (6 pack)
1. Cyberterrorism. I. Title.
HV6773.C4775 2010
363.325—dc22

2009022352

Manufactured in Malaysia

CPSIA Compliance Information: Batch #TWW10YA: For Further Information contact Rosen Publishing, New York, New York at 1-800-237-9932

On the cover: Hacking ranges from merely mischievous behavior to dangerous, destructive, and terroristic activity. Yet any attempts to break into a server or computer system, regardless of one's intent, is a crime and therefore punishable by law.

CONTENTS

Introduction

Imagine this scenario: The lights go out, and you look outside the window. It's clear that no one has electricity for miles around. You pick up the phone. It's dead. So is the cell phone. All communications have been cut off.

At a nearby hospital, emergency generators produce a dim light in the hallways. Even with the generators, the computers aren't responding. A virus has corrupted the system. Doctors' pagers are going haywire. The intensive care unit is shut down. Nurses run up and down the halls carrying charts, no longer able to send or receive medical information electronically. Patients wait for many long hours to receive medicine and treatment as the chaos spreads and the hospital's usual systems and procedures break down.

Suddenly, an explosion can be heard in the distance. And then another one. Without television, radio, telephones, or Internet access, no one knows what's going on. Has the city been attacked? What about the nuclear plant across the river? Everyone is thrown into a state of confusion, fear, and panic. With

A major power outage in 2003 conjured fears of cyberterrorism. Electrical grids interconnect cities across the country—powering lights, computers, refrigeration, emergency response systems, and so on—making them an obvious target for terrorist attacks.

communications down, no one can be reached—not the police, not the firefighters, not the FBI.

When people think of cyberterrorism, this is the kind of scenario that is called to mind: a total systems shutdown. An unseen enemy. It's the stuff of Hollywood movies and sensational novels.

Cyberterrorism hinges on the widespread use of computers by individuals, private industry and corporations, the military, and the government and its agencies. Not long ago, there was no such thing as a personal computer. Now we are all attached to our electronic devices and, through them, the vastness of cyberspace. At no time in history has information ever been so accessible to the individual—or so vulnerable to attack by a single crafty terrorist armed with just a computer and an Internet connection.

Like anything of value, information can be stolen, corrupted, or destroyed. In spite of developments in encryption (protective coding), firewalls (barriers to unauthorized access), and other security systems, there is always the threat of criminals hacking through a computer network's security system from any location in the world, no matter how remote.

But how likely is a widespread cyberattack that cripples not only an individual's computer or a company's network, but whole communities, cities, or even nations? Are we prepared? Is it possible to be prepared for such an invisible, undefined enemy?

What makes the prospect of a large-scale, devastating cyberattack so believable is that hacking occurs regularly and with apparent ease. Most hacking incidents turn out to be pranks. For example, the Twitter pages of Barack Obama and Britney Spears were hacked into in 2009, and the hackers posted false and inappropriate messages.

Yet much hacking activity is far more serious, sinister, and potentially dangerous than silly attention-seeking stunts. In 2002, a British man named Gary McKinnon was accused of hacking into almost one hundred U.S. military computers, as well as the National Aeronautics and Space Administration (NASA) computer system. He claimed to have been looking for proof of alien life. He faced seventy years in prison. His mother said, "He's not a genius. He's good, but he's not the best. They had no passwords, no firewalls, and that's the problem" (as quoted in the TimesOnline, UK). The U.S. military estimated the cost of McKinnon's cyberspace break-in at close to $1 billion (the cost of tracking and correcting the problems he caused while hacking).

The hospital scenario that was described earlier in this chapter actually occurred to a lesser degree in November 2008. Three hospitals in London, England, were infected by a computer virus called Mytob. The hospitals were St. Bartholomew's, the Royal London Hospital, and the London Chest Hospital. Mytob spreads via e-mail. It plants a computer virus that allows hackers to wreak havoc on a system, including shutting out its users. The London hospitals immediately assured the public that "well-rehearsed emergency procedures have been activated to ensure that key clinical systems continue while network access is being established" (as quoted by ComputerWeekly). What this meant, among other things, was that doctors went back to using pen and paper.

How likely is it that a disastrous chain of events will really play out in the way discussed here? Is there any way to stop or prevent cyberterrorism? Or are we doomed to be thrust back into the relative dark ages of the pre-digital era in the blink of an eye—or the click of a mouse?

Chapter 1

CYBERATTACKERS AND THEIR TECHNIQUES

Kevin Mitnick, a notorious hacker who had broken into many corporate and university computer systems, is seen here being released from federal prison.

A report released in December 2008 by the Commission of Cyber Security for the Forty-Fourth Presidency stressed that "cybersecurity is now one of the major national security problems facing the United States." Ever since the terrorist attacks of September 11, 2001, Americans have been increasingly sensitive to and anxious about the vulnerability of the nation's computer systems. These systems are a tempting target that seems easily accessible to terrorists who could exploit them to achieve their destructive goals—mainly the spreading of fear and mayhem.

Terrorism: Striking Fear Where We Live

Terrorism is the use of violence by irregular combatants (those who are not members of a formal national army) to intimidate and frighten civilian populations and send a political message. It differs from traditional military tactics in one particular and very important way: civilians are often targeted. Terrorists do not distinguish between civilians and military combatants. Civilians are seen as being active participants in and supporters of the power structure and social system that the terrorists are against. They are seen as guilty parties, rather than innocent victims. In fact, terrorists often plan acts of violence that will result in mass civilian casualties.

The terrorist attacks of 9/11 are horrific examples of this. Most of the more than two thousand victims that day were civilians. The carefully coordinated attacks came with little advance warning. The attackers, members of the radical Islamic terrorist group Al Qaeda, were not part of any formal army, nor did they fight on behalf of any particular nation.

During the second half of the twentieth century, the United States had one primary and obvious enemy: the Soviet Union. Following the end of the Cold War and the collapse of the Soviet Empire, the United States enjoyed a brief period of confidence and false security, believing that because it was the only remaining superpower, there were no enemies out there who could inflict much harm. That illusion was shattered on 9/11. It turned out that the enemy was invisible, elusive, and able to strike any American citizen, territory, or installation anywhere in the world, including at home. Suddenly, no American felt safe—not at work, not at the mall, not even at home.

Vague Threats and an Invisible Enemy

It's not hard to imagine scenarios in which cyberterrorism could be the perfect vehicle to create mass casualties and random civilian victimization. Terrorists look for weaknesses that they can exploit. With the 9/11 attacks, it was the U.S. airline system and its lax security procedures. It's possible that the next weak spot terrorists identify will be in one of our computer systems. This approach gives them the anonymity they value, as well as the potential for massive damage with a huge psychological impact. "The next generation of terrorists will grow up in a digital world, with ever more powerful and easy-to-use hacking tools at their disposal," said Dorothy Denning, a professor of defense analysis at the Naval Postgraduate School in California and a leading cybersecurity expert, in her article "Is Cyber Terror Next?"

It's difficult to identify enemies who might use terrorist or cyberterrorist tactics. There are many nongovernmental foreign militant groups like Al Qaeda. There are also domestic (homegrown) terrorists like Timothy McVeigh, who bombed a federal building in Oklahoma City in 1995, killing 168 people, including nineteen small children in day care. Groups like Al Qaeda already use the Internet to spread messages of hate and violence. The threats are often unspecified—terrorists' motives are not simply to destroy property, but to cause psychological trauma. The mere act of spreading fear through vague threats is a terrorist act and achieves the terrorists' main goal.

Although there are no documented acts of significant cyberterrorism against the United States, there is evidence

The National Cyber Security Division's operational arm, the U.S. Computer Emergency Readiness Team (US-CERT; accessed via http://www.us-cert.gov), coordinates public and private sector responses to cyberattacks.

that Al Qaeda has searched online for weak spots. Experience tells us that our computer systems are vulnerable to attack. Security breaches have troubled the government for years. The Department of Homeland Security's U.S. Computer Emergency Readiness Team (US-CERT) reports that there were 18,050 computer breaches in government agencies in 2008, more than three times as many than in 2006. One example occurred over the July 4 holiday weekend in 2009, when fourteen major Web sites in the United States—including those of the White House, the State Department, and the New York Stock Exchange—came under attack. Blame was initially placed on North Korean hackers, who were possibly government-supported. This increase in cyberattacks is attributed to the fact that hackers now have greater access to malicious software, or malware.

Types of Cyberattacks

Documented cases of cybervulnerability and cyberattacks fall into one of five categories: system flaws, cybercrime, hacktivism, cyberwarfare, and pranks.

System Flaw: Y2K

The ultimate example of a system flaw was the year 2000 problem. The problem was also known as the Millennium Bug, or Y2K. As 2000 approached, people's attention was drawn to a glitch in early computer program design that used only two digits to represent years. For example, the year 1990 was coded as 90, the year 1995 as 95, and so on. This was done to save programming time and costs.

The fear was that after 2000, computer processors and software that used the two-digit code would stop moving forward. Instead, they would recognize 00 as 1900. Dire warnings spread that, since computers run electrical systems, the whole world would go dark at midnight on January 1, 2000. Further chaos would ensue as money in the stock market would disappear because those monies were not around in 1900. Investors would be penniless, at least in the electronic world.

Governments, private companies and corporations, and ordinary citizens spent billions of dollars reprogramming their systems. They raced against the clock to complete the corrections by midnight at the turn of the millennium. (Some have estimated that the cost of Y2K-related computer assessment and repair was $1 trillion or more.) People even bought or created "Y2K kits" that contained flashlights, batteries, canned food, blankets, bottled water, cash, and other short-term survival aids. This was in case a major electronic shutdown occurred, cutting off access to light, heat, refrigeration, and bank accounts.

On January 1, 2000, some problems were reported, but none endangered the public. In Ishikawa, Japan, radiation-monitoring equipment simply stopped working at midnight, but the malfunction was quickly detected and fixed. In Washington, D.C., the U.S. Naval Observatory's master clock, which keeps the country's official time, reported incorrectly that the date was January 1, 19100. In Delaware, 150 slot machines at racetracks stopped working. In the final analysis, it seems none of the countries that didn't bother to prepare for the Millennium Bug, such as Italy, China, and Russia, experienced any Y2K problems worth reporting, and that the whole incident was overblown.

Cybercrime

Cybercrime includes the use of a computer to commit fraud, distribute obscene or offensive content, or engage in harassment. Obscene or offensive content is not protected by the First Amendment of the U.S. Constitution, which safeguards one's right to free speech. Obscene or offensive content includes written, oral, and visual forms of self-expression that are racist, blasphemous, subversive, or incite hate

Owen Thor Walker, a teen hacker, was hired by a large telecommunications company as its security consultant, although he had been charged with several computer crimes estimated to have caused some $20 million worth of damage.

crimes. It is also against the law to send spam, which is unsolicited junk e-mail.

For several months in 2008, a Massachusetts couple harassed their neighbors in retaliation over a land dispute. They tried to open up bank accounts using their neighbors' personal information, signed them up for membership at a nudist camp, filed false reports of child abuse to local child welfare authorities, and more. All of these acts are cybercrimes. The couple was charged with harassment, conspiracy, and identity fraud.

Another example of cybercrime involves an eighteen-year-old New Zealander named Owen Thor Walker. He was the mastermind behind a cybergang that managed to infect more than a million computers around the world. Authorities said that Walker and his crew managed to steal bank and credit card information and manipulate stock trades. The botnet they released may have stolen as much as $20 million worldwide. (A botnet is a software robot that runs automatically. Botnets are usually computers that have been infected by Internet viruses or worms and run malicious software that is controlled by the virus's creators.)

Hacktivism

Hacktivism is the use of computers to achieve social or political goals. Hacktivists want to protest or send a message, just as any activist does. Rather than march in the streets or organize boycotts and protests, however, they attack the Web sites of organizations they oppose. For example, antiglobalization hacktivists crippled the Web sites of the World Trade Organization.

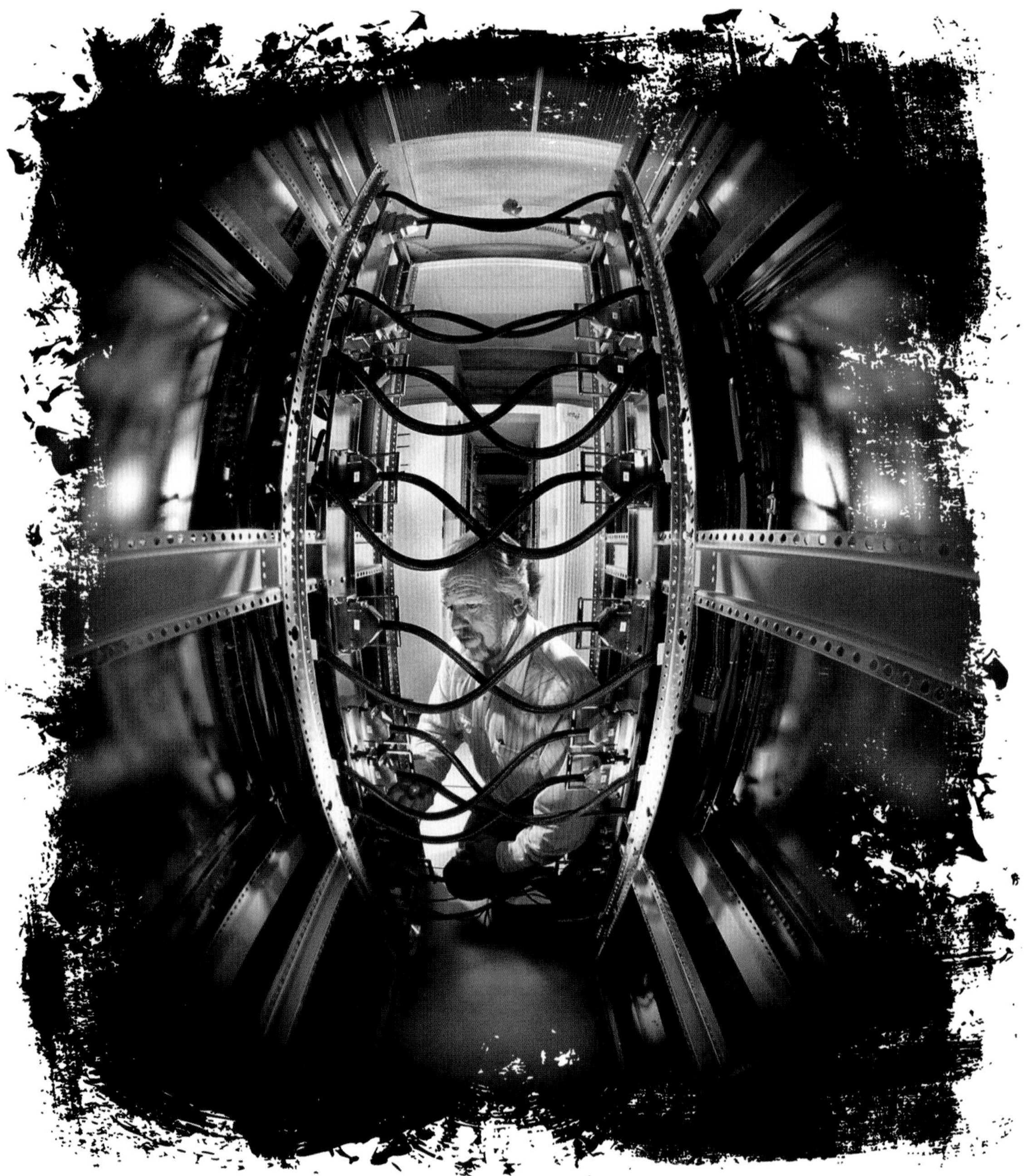

Sandia National Laboratories, where the components for nuclear weapons are developed, was once among several targets of cyberattacks. Within less than twenty minutes, the attackers stole valuable data and erased their tracks.

Cyberwarfare

Cyberwarfare is the use of computers and the Internet to conduct hostile acts, usually between two states. Although Al Qaeda is not a state but a militant terrorist organization, its use of the Internet to spread hate propaganda can be categorized as cyberwarfare. A good example of cyberwarfare is Titan Rain. This is what the U.S. government called the series of attacks, beginning in 2003, on American computer systems at places like NASA and Sandia National Laboratories, where the components for nuclear weapons are developed.

The Titan Rain attacks seem to have originated in China. In November 2008, a congressional panel warned that cyberattacks from China had increased by a third since the year before and that there were 250 hacker groups in China. "Vast amounts of sensitive information" have already been stolen, reported the panel. The Chinese government has denied any involvement in these attacks. It's not clear whether China's cyberspies are state-sponsored or independent, government agents or rogue individuals. The attackers may be trying to gather industrial information or just testing their ability to break into a rival nation's military system. Many countries, including China, are home to young computer programmers who are hacking simply "for fun" to test their abilities. Nevertheless, when their targets are the Central Intelligence Agency (CIA) or National Security Administration (NSA), it gives U.S. officials cause for concern.

Pranks and Cheating

The last category of documented cyberattacks involves pranksters and cheaters who, though not a threat to national security, can still cause a lot of damage and disruption. Included in this last category are two California students, Tanvir Singh and Omar Khan. Prosecutors charge that in 2008, Khan changed grades for a dozen students, including himself. The teens faced serious jail time. Khan could have received thirty-eight years in prison if convicted on all of the charges against him. Singh faced three years in jail.

Even relatively harmless pranks can cost a person jail time. Kevin Poulsen was already a fugitive from the law for hacking into government and military security systems. In 1990, he heard that a Los Angeles radio station was giving away a Porsche to the 102nd caller. He made sure he was that caller by taking control of the entire city's telephone network. Poulsen received a three-year sentence for his crime.

Hackers and Crackers

Many hackers are no more than curious amateur programmers. This was the case with "MafiaBoy," which was the Internet alias of Michael Calce, a high school student in Montreal, Canada. In 2000, he hacked into some of the largest Internet sites in the world, including Yahoo!, Amazon, CNN, Dell, and eBay. Calce launched denial-of-service attacks against these sites. Such attacks usually involve flooding Web sites with so many communication requests that the sites are overwhelmed in trying to respond to them. This results in very slow or unsuccessful loading of the sites for legitimate users. Often, the sites crash and are taken offline for a time. In court, Calce expressed the desire to move to Italy because of its lax computer crime laws.

"Cracker" is another word describing a hacker who breaches computer security, whether to steal information, disrupt or destroy computer systems, support a political cause, or test his or her hacking skills. Some hackers are computer security experts who are paid by the government or private corporations to test their security systems by seeing how easily they can break in using various tools and techniques to avoid detection. Some of these security experts are former criminal hackers, or, like Kevin Poulsen, engage in criminal hacking during or after their legitimate employment.

Today, crackers have more and better tools and techniques at their disposal. Cyberattacks can include these various forms of malware:

- Viruses (malicious programs that arrive in file attachments and damage a computer's hardware, software, and files)
- Worms (malicious programs that replicate themselves and travel from computer to computer by, for example, sending themselves to everyone in your e-mail address book)
- Trojan horses (malicious software that looks like legitimate software but, once installed on a computer, can delete files and destroy information)
- Phishing (fraudulent e-mails that look like legitimate correspondence from reputable banks, social networking sites, and online auction sites that seek to persuade you to provide sensitive personal information, such as bank account and credit card numbers, Social Security numbers, user names, and passwords)
- Denial-of-service attacks
- Control system attacks (attacks on the computer systems that control a nation's infrastructure, such

The Fight Against Spammers

On December 16, 2003, U.S. president George W. Bush signed the CAN-SPAM Act of 2003 into law. It was the first national law to regulate the sending of unsolicited commercial e-mails, or spam. CAN-SPAM is an acronym that stands for "Controlling the Assault of Non-Solicited Pornography and Marketing." The law requires senders of commercial e-mail to include a post office box or private mailbox and an "unsubscribe" link in all e-mails.

as dams and water supplies, electrical transmission networks, telephone and communication networks, and railroads)

The Code Red Worm and Other Malicious Cyberattacks

When malware enters the scene, it can cause widespread confusion. One form of malware is the computer worm, which is a program that spreads by attacking other computers and copying itself onto them. The resulting flood of data can cause performance slowdown or a complete shutdown of some parts of the Internet. In 2001, a computer worm called Code Red infected the U.S. Treasury Department's Financial Management Service (FMS). It deleted files and caused slow performance and system instability. The FMS was forced to pull the plug on its Web sites. As a result of the same worm, customers of Qwest, a telecommunications

Code Red alert

The computer worm "Code Red" operates on a monthly cycle that proliferates on Microsoft operating systems and may slow the Internet.

1 Day 1 - 19: Worm scans Internet, identifies vulnerable systems and infects them
- Each newly installed worm repeats process, causing scanning rate to grow rapidly; this causes Internet slowdown

2 Day 20 - 27: Attacks a predetermined IP address (e.g. the White House)

3 28 - end of month: Lies dormant until beginning of next month, when infected servers send out new data attacks

Who is affected?

- It attacks mainly Microsoft ISS Web servers. Vulnerable systems must be rebooted and Microsoft's patch for Code Red installed
- All Internet users may feel the effect: Slower Internet, blackouts, defaced Web pages

© 2001 KRT Source: Cert, McAfee, CNN Graphic: Ulla Knudsen, Morten Lyhne

In 2001, a computer worm called Code Red spread across the Internet. The worm deleted files and slowed down computer systems, affecting 750,000 computers worldwide.

carrier, lost digital subscriber line (DSL) coverage for ten days. The White House's Internet address was also targeted for a denial-of-service attack. The Code Red worm affected more than 750,000 computers worldwide.

In the wake of Code Red and other similar worms, air traffic control systems, utility networks, emergency response systems, and national defense systems seemed suddenly vulnerable to crippling attack. The increased role of information technology (IT), which now encompasses every aspect of our lives, particularly e-commerce (online banking, retailing, and networking), makes cyberterrorism a real threat to the economy.

The World Wide Web has millions of entry points and just as many infrastructure and software vulnerabilities. Yet its greatest vulnerability may be the human factor. Manipulating and deceiving people to gain confidential information is called social engineering. The master of social engineering is Kevin Mitnick, a hacker who eluded the Federal Bureau of Investigation (FBI) for two-and-a-half years in the mid-1990s. He broke into the computer systems of top technology companies like Fujitsu, Nokia, Motorola, and Sun Microsystems. In his book *The Art of Deception*, Mitnick says, "I could often get passwords and other pieces of sensitive information from companies by pretending to be someone else and just asking for it." He says that it is much easier to trick someone into giving you a password than to hack into the system.

It's no wonder then that online theft costs $1 trillion a year worldwide, according to experts at the World Economic Forum in Davos, Switzerland. The Code Red worm alone was estimated to have caused $2.6 billion in damage to computer networks.

Chapter 2

CYBERTERRORISM: WORST-CASE SCENARIOS

The word "cyberterrorism" brings to mind a shutdown that could cause Hollywood-style chaos in real life. Science-fiction novels and movies have made scenes of blacked-out cities and total social breakdown eerily familiar.

The threat of cyberterrorism triggers our worst fears. Most of us use computers every day to perform both professional and personal tasks. We know that so much of the world is connected to and controlled with the help of computers: banks, stock markets, the military, hospitals, electrical systems, nuclear power plants, and missile silos. The Internet has always been vulnerable. But as we get more connected to and reliant on it, we fear that an attack on the Internet could cripple the whole economy and even threaten national and international security.

It isn't hard to imagine disastrous scenarios relating to computer system vulnerabilities. The connection between computer networks and criminal activity is never far from our consciousness, whether when being spooked by sci-fi and techno thrillers or sitting before the monitors of our real-world computers, carefully avoiding spam e-mail and file attachments from unknown senders.

This fear is not irrational or misplaced. In fact, real cause for fear is increasing each year. "The United States was not routinely targeted by terrorists until 1982," says Jonathan R. White in *Terrorism: An Introduction*. Since then, an entire industry has grown out of our fears of terrorism and attempts to defend against it. Cyberterrorism, in particular, has become a growth area for think tanks like the Potomac Institute, which conducts research on issues of national security and the role of security consultants and IT specialists. As Dan Verton points out in *Black Ice*, an investigative look at cyberterrorism, no one could have imagined attacks like the ones on 9/11, despite the occurrence of earlier, lesser terrorist attacks like the bombing of the World Trade Center in 1993. Even as cameras captured the first plane crashing into the World Trade Center on the morning of 9/11, people initially believed it was just an accident. In the same way, Verton warns, we may not recognize the looming threat of an imminent cyberattack.

Security experts try to anticipate when, where, and how a future cyberattack might come. Perhaps terrorists might use a virus to snarl the taxpayer database of the Internal Revenue Service (IRS). Or as Richard Clarke, former White House advisor on cyberterrorism with the U.S. Department of Homeland Security, warns, they might tamper with the control systems

Hacker-Cons

Each year, hacker conventions take place around the world. The largest of these "hacker-cons" is DEFCON, in Las Vegas, Nevada. SummerCon is one of the oldest. Another, Black Hat, calls itself "the world's premier technical security conference." Who attends? Mostly computer security professionals, government employees, lawyers, and, of course, hackers. Anyone interested in computer code and design will find these conventions intriguing and worthwhile.

of the power supply infrastructure. They may then disable "electrical power grids and telephones as surely as if they had been destroyed" (as quoted in Declan McCullough's *Wired* article "The Sentinel").

Identifying the Enemy Among Us

One of the difficulties facing security experts is identifying where a cyberthreat might come from. Although 9/11 turned our attention toward transnational terrorists from Muslim countries, there has always been political violence in America's domestic history. If the country experiences a cyberattack, it is just as likely to come from homegrown American extremists, such as antigovernment militias, hate groups, or radicals supporting a particular political cause.

During the 1980s, the United States experienced a wave of domestic terrorism: the bombing of nearly forty abortion clinics in different states. In the 1990s, militant antiabortion

After an eighteen-year manhunt, Theodore John Kaczynski, a former University of California at Berkeley math professor, was identified as the Unabomber. Kaczynski is now serving a life sentence.

attackers increased the number of arson and bombing incidents, adding the murder of individuals who worked at abortion clinics to their strategy. At least eight people have died in abortion clinic bombings, assassinations, or assaults, including Dr. George Tiller of Wichita, Kansas, in May 2009.

From 1978 until his arrest in 1996, Theodore Kaczynski, also known as the Unabomber, carried out a series of mail bombings that resulted in three deaths and twenty-three injuries. In 1995, he sent a letter to the *New York Times* in which he promised to "desist from terrorism" if the *Times* or the *Washington Post* published his antitechnology manifesto.

As history and these examples show, terrorist attacks can come from unexpected places. That element of surprise—and the shock and fear that it creates—is one of the main tactics of a terrorist. Even the most unlikely political causes and the least suspicious people can inspire violent and horrific attacks. For example, members of the Animal Liberation Front (ALF), a militant animal rights protest group, have committed deadly acts of terrorism. And we have already discussed the case of the U.S. Army veteran and security guard Timothy McVeigh, who blew up a federal building in Oklahoma.

Knowing where a truly destructive cyberattack will come from is as difficult as knowing where the next conventional terrorist strike will come from. It is also unclear if cyberattacks will come from more traditional terrorist groups like Al Qaeda, or from an entirely new—and as yet unknown—breed of cyberterrorists.

Attacking Control Systems

Many experts believe it won't take much for chaos to erupt. Most critical infrastructure in Western countries is networked through computers. In the United States, these control systems are known as SCADA, or supervisory control and data acquisition, systems. They are obvious targets. SCADA systems are vital because they manage physical processes. They throw switches, shut valves, adjust temperatures, and regulate pressure. They are used in vital industries, including electric power, oil and gas refining and pipelines, water treatment and distribution, chemical production and processing, railroads and mass transit, and manufacturing. There are a growing number of connections between SCADA systems,

In the United States, most critical infrastructure is networked through computers. They are used in vital industries, including electric power. Technicians monitor these systems in control rooms such as this one.

office networks, and the Internet. This makes them vulnerable to attacks and thus worries a lot of security researchers.

Think of natural gas distribution. Computers monitor and control the pressure and flow of gas through pipelines. If a cyberterrorist who has hacked into the system instructs the computer to shut down the flow of gas, the pressure in the pipelines could build up to a dangerous level, causing an explosion.

Here's another scary scenario: imagine that the computers of a major pharmaceutical company are the target. A cyberterrorist could tamper with the control system enough to interfere with the production process of a drug. The result would be a defective product, perhaps containing toxic levels of a drug. Or the product could contain too little of the drug to be effective and manage a patient's life-threatening illness. Then the cyberterrorist would tamper with the quality control system so that the defect would not be noticed.

A life-saving drug could be produced with the wrong levels of active ingredients, causing the death or disability of thousands of people before the tampering is noticed. As more people learn of this, panic would quickly spread. In theory, any attack on the control systems of essential services—like water and fuel supplies, transportation, electricity, and health care—threatens public health and safety and is therefore a threat to national security.

Disrupting Internet Traffic

The Internet's major hubs are also tempting targets for cyberterrorists. These hubs are found in major cities where the equipment that collects and distributes Internet traffic is located. A cyberattack on a major hub could disrupt Internet functions and disconnect smaller cities linked to the Internet via that hub.

Security experts worry that a malicious programmer might bring the entire Web down with a virus like Slammer, which spread around the world in 2003. This worm randomly and aggressively searched for victims. It targeted five of the Internet's thirteen major hubs. One of these was a major telecommunications hub located at Ground Zero (site of the former World Trade Center) in New York City. Three New York counties were disconnected from New York State's computer system, and several major Internet services and e-business providers were knocked out for almost two days.

Malware

There are many forms of malware, software that is designed to infiltrate and damage computer systems. They include computer viruses, worms, or Trojan horses. Spyware intercepts or takes partial control of users' interactions with their computer. Rootkits hide the fact that a system has been compromised. Crimeware steals money automatically.

A single virus could disrupt our daily activities. Imagine if thousands of Web pages suddenly went blank, only to be replaced by the error message "404-Not Found." Thousands of popular Web sites, from Facebook to YouTube, are replaced by malicious messages. Tens of millions of dollars are wiped off the share price of companies. News broadcasts start announcing that hundreds of thousands of personal bank accounts have been raided overnight. Soon, people make a run on their banks, angrily demanding their savings in cash. The rapid withdrawal of cash leads to a shortage of notes and coins. Meanwhile, the computer virus spreads to air

Malware is software designed to break into and damage computer systems. A program that replaced thousands of Web pages with an error like this one could cause millions of dollars in damage.

traffic control systems, causing deadly midair collisions between passenger jets carrying hundreds of people each. By the time the virus is finally destroyed, thousands of people are dead. The country will spend years and billions of dollars repairing the damage and recovering from the devastation that was wreaked online and off.

These are some of the common scenarios that people think of when cyberterrorism is mentioned. Some experts suggest that these worst-case scenarios are quite possible, while others argue that they are just the product of very active imaginations. Something that is of concern for the U.S. government is terrorists coordinating cyberattacks with physical ones to create an overwhelming chain of cascading disasters—with limited or no ability to respond to them. Just think, for example, how much worse 9/11 would have been if the terrorists had also hacked into and disrupted emergency response services, the power grid, phone and Internet communications, and transportation systems. This is the kind of worst-case scenario that keeps government officials and intelligence agents up at night, precisely because they are convinced of its plausibility.

Chapter 3

HOW REAL IS THE THREAT?

Two men monitor the flow of interstate traffic in a highway operations center. Cyberattacks upon American infrastructure are a major concern for the nation's defense, homeland security, and intelligence communities.

It appears that the number of breaches on U.S. computer systems is increasing, as is the destructive use of the Internet. For example, the Internet is increasingly being used for posting hate-filled, threatening messages, pictures, and video, often on hacked and hijacked Web sites. There have also been cybercrimes that were politically motivated. Do these breaches really amount to cyberterrorism? That depends on your definition of cyberterrorism.

The FBI defines cyberterrorism as a "premeditated, politically motivated attack against information, computers, computer programs, and data that results in violence against noncombatant targets by subnational groups or clandestine agents." Noncombatants are civilians, citizens who are not members of an army or militia. Subnational groups are terrorist groups or militias that are not officially sanctioned by any national government but operate on their own, often in violation of the law and against established governments. "Clandestine agents" are secret agents—spies or intelligence operatives who work for legitimate governments, rebel organizations, or terrorist groups. The FBI's definition of cyberterrorism stresses that for hacking, vandalism, and tampering to rise to the level of cyberterrorism, they must result in violence against members of civilian society—or at least pose the potential for violent harm.

Security experts noted some 1,200 cyberattacks were politically motivated following the midair collision of a U.S. spy plane and a Chinese fighter jet in April 2001. Targets of these angry acts of cyberretaliation and protest included the U.S. Air Force, the Department of Energy, and the White House. Perpetrators defaced Web sites with pro-Chinese images or launched denial-of-service attacks. Although these actions did have a financial cost (in lost productivity, repairing the systems, etc.), there was no loss of lives or threatened or actual violence.

The Hype: Spreading Fear, Reducing Risk

The media tends to feed on the public's anxiety and paranoia. Threats to computer systems make headlines. An Associated Press article titled "Conficker Worm Set to Spring to Life"

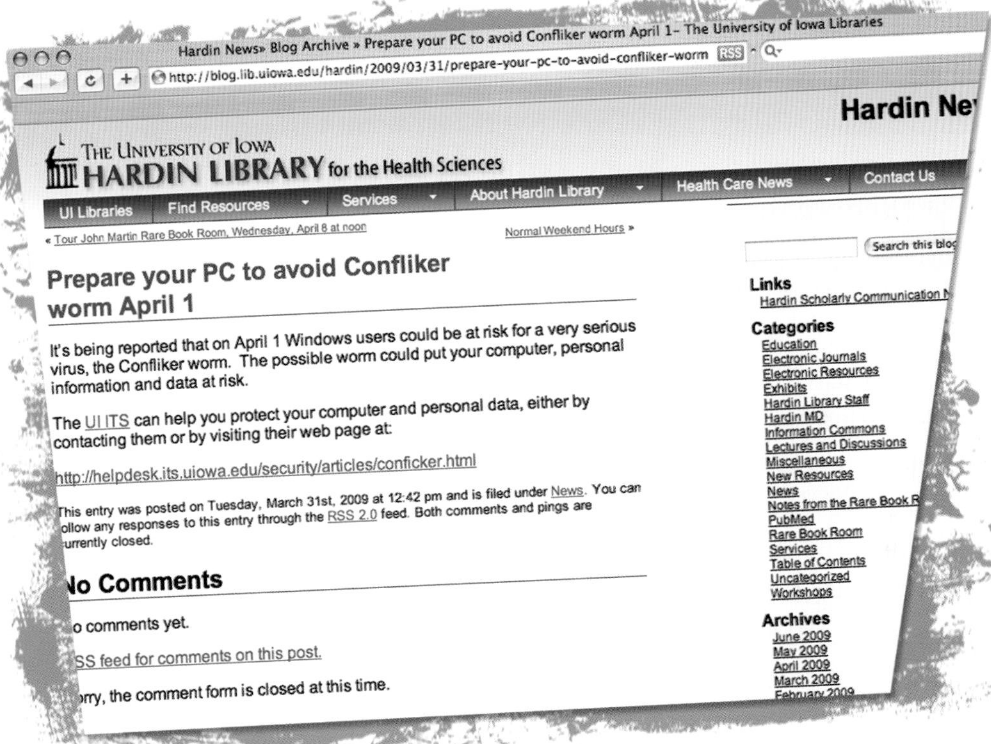

The media warned of damage from a worm, Conficker, planned for April 1, 2009. This warning was posted by the Hardin Library of the University of Iowa (http://www.lib.uiowa.edu/hardin), but the day passed without incident.

warned of a worm planned for April Fool's Day, 2009. This article said that Conficker "could cause havoc, from massive network outages to the creation of a cyberweapon of mass destruction that attacks government computers." Conficker would infect millions of computers and would steal passwords, credit card data, and banking information, reported various media outlets.

But even as these words were written, researchers felt that, as with previous malware, the day would pass without any catastrophic harm or extensive damage. They were proved to be correct. The fact was that Conficker first appeared in October 2008, at which time it infected millions of personal computers (PCs). Just how many millions is not known. Conficker gained so much publicity in the following months that researchers and companies focused their attention on it and were quickly able to identify its programming flaws. Microsoft patched the security hole in Windows, which Conficker used to get in, and software manufacturers developed Conficker removal tools.

The Conficker story illustrates how important secrecy is to a hacker's success. In order to carry out an effective cyberattack, hackers need stealth, not publicity. This is contrary to the goals of conventional terrorists, who try to get the entire world's attention by making wild threats and occasionally following through on them. As we have seen, the Conficker worm was largely defeated by its own publicity. "I think the threat was genuine," says Alfred Huger, a security response executive at Symantec. "And without all the attention, it could have been a big problem."

The Gap Between Fear and Reality

Amid all the fear of cyberterrorism, some people point out that there have been no actual reports of infiltration of computer systems that has resulted in violence or physical danger. As of yet, there is no credible evidence revealing that Al Qaeda or any other terrorist organization is planning a cyber assault. Probably, the reason is that the possibility of causing death on a large scale through such an assault is slim to none.

Terrorists want to create spectacular events that bring attention to their cause, such as 9/11, the March 2004 Madrid train bombings, and the July 2005 attacks against London's transit system. Unless a cyberterrorist can hack into several major computer systems at once, seize control of large sections of a country's infrastructure and defense control systems, and unleash utter chaos in its water, energy, communications, transit, and weapons systems, the likelihood of widespread and massive death or injury is unlikely.

Experts believe that to pull off an effective attack on the nation's infrastructure, cyberterrorists would need to have more than just the ability to crack the computer system. They would also need to have enormous technical knowledge about, say, a plant's mechanical functions and how to exploit them. This is not information that is easily acquired. This argument goes back to the reality that it would be much easier for a terrorist to send a powerful message with physical attacks and crude explosives than through high-tech and expert sabotage. "Not only does [cyberterrorism] not rank alongside chemical, biological, or nuclear weapons, but it is not anywhere near as serious as other potential threats like car bombs or suicide bombers," says bioterrorism expert Dorothy Denning.

In a way, actual cyberterrorism has not caught up to the fear of cyberterrorism. In 1998, it was reported that the computers controlling the floodgates of the Theodore Roosevelt Dam in Arizona had been hacked into. The hacker was a twelve-year-old boy. If he had opened the floodgates, reports said, walls of water could have flooded the cities of Tempe and Mesa, affecting nearly one million people. This is a terrifying prospect for sure, but the problem with this story is that it isn't true. It turned out to be an urban myth based on an actual, but far less, dramatic hacking incident involving an Arizona water facility and a twenty-seven-year-old perpetrator.

In 1998, reports that computers controlling the Theodore Roosevelt Dam had been hacked into proved false. The possibility remains that dams, like the Hoover Dam pictured above, and other infrastructure could be vulnerable to attacks.

People have always had a distrust of computer technology. And when things go wrong, it is easy for them to imagine the worst. During the Northeast Blackout of 2003, less than two years after 9/11, many people immediately assumed there had been a terrorist attack. It was a widespread power outage that stretched through parts of the northeastern and midwestern United States to Ontario, Canada. Even after the lights went back on, there continued to be incorrect media reports and Internet speculation that foreign hackers were behind the blackout, as well as a second widespread blackout in Florida in 2008. Many of these rumors blamed Chinese government-supported hackers.

The power outages were actually caused by faulty, aging infrastructure and human error. The North American Electric Reliability Corporation (NERC), an organization of U.S. electrical grid operators, investigated the 2003 blackout and concluded that a series of events contributed to the cascading blackout. First, the utility company FirstEnergy failed to cut back trees that were growing onto high-voltage power lines in Ohio. When branches caught the power lines, they tripped. A chain of bad decisions and communication failures followed. Within minutes, much of the Northeast was plunged into darkness. And it could easily happen again, without the help of cyberterrorists. "[T]he U.S. ranks toward the bottom among developed nations in terms of reliability of its electricity service," according to a report from Carnegie Mellon University. The report goes on to say that the average U.S. electric utility customer experiences 214 minutes of power outage a year, compared to only seventy in Great Britain and six in Japan.

Blaming foreign spies for these kinds of system failures shows how terrified we are of the potential for cyberterrorism. Yet because our fear outpaces the actual incidence of

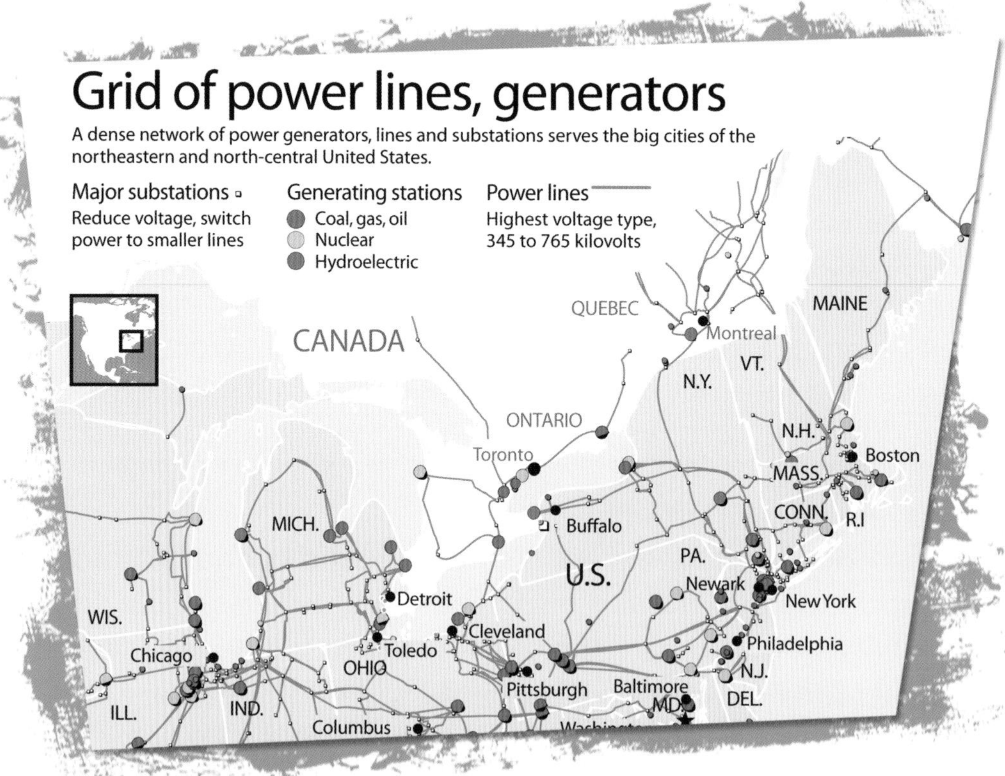

This map shows transmission lines, power plants, and substations for the northeastern United States, the north-central states, and southern Canada. Faulty, aging equipment caused a blackout of this grid in 2003.

cyberattacks, we are staying one step ahead of the game. We are remaining vigilant and putting defenses in place that help thwart or deter the very thing we are most afraid of. Indeed, to some extent the apparent increase in computer crime is due in part to the fact that government agencies have improved their ability to detect and report breaches to computer systems. The number of breaches, hacking, and other computer crimes may not actually be rising significantly. But their detection is, which is great news for all of us.

Blackout!

The Northeast Blackout of 2003 was the largest electrical blackout in history. It took place on Thursday, August 14, 2003, at 4:15 PM Eastern Standard Time (EST). It affected approximately ten million people in Ontario, Canada, and forty million people in eight U.S. states in the Northeast and Midwest. Power was restored in most places by the next day. The U.S. power grid is expecting an upgrade to "smart grids" by 2012.

Cyberterrorism or Merely an Expensive Nuisance?

In 2008, more than thirty-five million data breaches were reported in the United States. But how many of these are really serious? Some estimate that billions of dollars in damage have resulted from computer worms like Code Red. But since there is no way to calculate the cost accurately, many feel that these figures are hugely exaggerated.

Even hackers have a code of ethics. Most hackers, as opposed to malicious cyberterrorists bent on violent disruption and destruction, believe that cracking into a system for fun and exploration is all right as long as they don't commit a crime or cause any harm. Hackers often see themselves as free spirits and believe that sharing information is a positive thing and redistributes power. "Although hackers have the knowledge, skills, and tools to attack computer systems, they generally lack the motivation to cause violence or severe economic or social harm," says Denning. According to him, "Attacks that disrupt nonessential services or that are mainly a costly nuisance" do not count as cyberterrorism.

Dire warnings of cyberattacks come easily from the government and security experts. In the event of an attack, government agencies don't want to be caught off guard, as they were on 9/11. As for security experts, they stand to gain from pointing out the vulnerabilities of the Internet. Although the fear of cyberterrorism may be exaggerated, we can't afford to ignore its genuine threat. It is always a possibility that the success of the West's "war on terror" can make frustrated conventional terrorists turn to unconventional weapons, such as cyberterrorism. As a new, more computer-savvy generation of terrorists comes of age, the danger seems set to increase.

Chapter 4

FIGHTING CYBERATTACKS AND CYBERTERRORISM

More and more sophisticated methods of computer protection are available to consumers today. Antivirus programs, firewalls, and encryption programs try to stay a step ahead of computer viruses and hackers.

Disaster stories, dire predictions, and worst-case scenarios make great news. That's a big part of why we are so aware of the potential for tragedy. In recent years, an increasing number of disaster scenarios have centered upon cyberterrorism. But many security experts disagree with the idea that the next terrorist attack will come over the Internet or through our nation's computer systems. Just as quickly as hackers can break into a system, security measures are being developed to defend the nation's computers. These frontline defenses include firewalls (part of a computer system or network designed to block unauthorized access), antivirus software, intrusion detection and prevention systems, and encryption (security coding).

Security Administrators

A secure computer system should have an experienced security administrator. Many computer breaches and system accidents or failures are caused, at least in part, by human error. A well-trained security administrator can prevent such incidents. He or she will run tests to search for possible entry points and weak spots in a network. This way, the security administrator will stay a step ahead of any cybercriminals. As soon as a vulnerable spot is identified, he or she will apply the necessary patches to close it up.

The security administrator will put in place security policies that must be made known to, and strictly followed by, all personnel. He or she will also set up mechanisms that continuously test and evaluate the system and network security. For example, the system will run scripts every hour to report any suspicious activities on the network. Sometimes, a computer system is connected to the Internet as a trap. It appears to be part of the network, but in fact, it is isolated and unprotected on purpose. These are called "honey pots." Any breaches of this dummy system are monitored, and information on how a cracker gets in and exploits a system is gathered.

An experienced security administrator can spot false alarms, which may be triggered by legitimate system users during their everyday computing activities. Being able to quickly distinguish between an external threatening breach and an innocent internal user or system error can keep the

ARPANET

ARPANET is the predecessor of today's Internet. "ARPA" stands for the Advanced Research Project Agency. It was developed by the U.S. Department of Defense during the Cold War. Some people think that ARPANET was designed as a central command system that would survive a nuclear attack. But the real reason it was built was that there were only a few large, powerful research computers at the time, and they were separated by geography. ARPANET used a new technology called packet switching to link these far-flung, isolated computers into a network, allowing them to communicate and share information with each other. ARPANET grew to include e-mail and file transfer. Eventually, it became just a part of the emerging Internet.

security administrator from being distracted from genuine threats and attacks.

Making Computer Systems Isolated and Inaccessible

In theory, cyberterrorists could disable military, financial, and telecommunications systems. However, nuclear weapons and other sensitive military systems, as well as the computer systems of the FBI and CIA, are "air-gapped," making them inaccessible to outside hackers. Systems in the private sector tend to be less well protected, but they are far from defenseless. Nightmarish tales of their vulnerability tend to be mere gossip and urban legends.

Critical infrastructure is more vulnerable to human error than to cyberterrorism. The Davis-Besse Nuclear Power Station in Ohio was shut down in 2003 after several operator errors were revealed.

When the Slammer worm spread through Microsoft software, it crippled two computer systems responsible for monitoring pressure and temperature during accidents at a nuclear power plant in Ohio. Slammer wasn't designed to

target the plant, however. It more or less accidentally infected it as it spread from computer to computer nationwide. It is important to note that these two computer systems were not critical systems. They weren't part of the nuclear power plant's safety systems. In fact, the Nuclear Regulatory Commission requires computers that are part of safety systems to be isolated and inaccessible.

Jeff Moss, organizer of the annual DEFCON computer hacker's convention, believes that terrorist groups like Al Qaeda are more likely to use bombs than to plan and successfully launch a massive cyberattack. Causing a nationwide computer meltdown would be like "trying to solve three hundred problems," Moss said to Michael S. James of ABC News. "Why spend all your time coming up with the most secretive, zero-day, computerized exploit when one guy with a hacksaw in a manhole could probably cause just as many problems?"

New Initiatives and Technologies

That doesn't mean that officials aren't trying to stay a step ahead of cyberterrorist threats. One step that President Barack Obama took was to start a two-month cyberspace policy review in order to determine how well the U.S. handles malicious hackers. One of the goals of this review was to identify new and improved cybersecurity strategies, as well as coordinate the security of military computer networks and develop offensive cyberweapons. In May 2009, President Obama announced the creation of a new "cyber-czar" position within the White House to combat what he said were constant attacks against American defense and military networks and more than $8 billion in losses related to cybercrimes committed against individuals and companies.

Meanwhile, researchers are developing the next generation of cybersecurity systems. At the U.S. Department of Energy's Oak Ridge National Laboratory in Oak Ridge, Tennessee, science fiction is becoming science fact. Scientists there are working on cybots, which are software robots designed to protect networks from intruders. Cybots will immediately be able to respond to threats and breaches, and collaborate with each other to prevent or halt an attack. Their speed will prevent hackers from using a diversion in one part of a computer system or network, while launching an actual attack elsewhere. "You give [the cybot] a mission and tools to work with, such as mobility and intrusion sensors, and it uses those tools and cooperates with other cybots to accomplish the mission," says project developer Lawrence MacIntyre in the article "Oak Ridge Explores Cybots." Cybots' missions may include monitoring systems, detecting intrusions, and managing data.

Numerous other security measures are being planned and implemented. Research and development is being done to create strong identification tools for computer control systems that are as successful as the Common Access Card, which employees must use to gain physical entry into sensitive facilities. For instance, better authentication methods for access to critical infrastructure are being developed, including digital

Iris-recognition technology is the latest breakthrough in computer security. It is more accurate than fingerprinting and other biometric markers. Markings in the iris are unique to each person and do not change.

certificates, smart cards, and biometric technologies like voice, retina, and fingerprint identification. A user would not be permitted to log on to a restricted computer or enter certain sensitive areas of the computer system or network if his or her voice, retina, or fingerprints, when scanned, did not provide a match with that of an authorized user.

Work is also being done on using federal regulations to give operators of critical infrastructure, such as electrical power plants, more incentive to secure their systems. One suggestion was to use the Obama administration's economic stimulus plan to require that companies invest in security. Other ideas include implementing the kind of well-coordinated campaign that characterized Y2K preparations. This would include widespread awareness-raising strategies and a "Y2K-style toolkit" to help countries assess their security risks and develop strategies to reduce that risk.

Low-Tech Solutions

Despite all of these high-tech initiatives and cutting-edge research and development, infiltration through the Internet may be best handled with a low-tech solution. First, training personnel in cybersafety is crucial. Furthermore, there are situations when it is better not to stop a hacker from breaking in. Instead, you silently track the hacker to see what his or her plan is, what his or her intentions or objectives seem to be, and where he or she is trying to go. In many instances, there is no need to even follow the intruder because it becomes clear that he or she doesn't intend to do any harm. Hackers are often just trying to gain free access to a computer and its network's communication resources.

In another sense, the low-tech approach is the answer to cybersecurity fears. One thing that keeps SCADA systems from being an easy target is that they are usually kept

Security experts have learned that it is sometimes better not to stop a hacker. Instead, they silently track the hacker. More often than not, hackers don't have criminal intentions but are motivated by simple curiosity.

separate from other systems. "They tend to be obscure, old-fashioned systems that are incompatible with Internet technology anyhow," says Tom Standage, technology editor at the *Economist* magazine, in the article "The Mouse that

Might Roar." "Even authorized users would require specialized knowledge."

Old-fashioned cooperation and community-mindedness can also help thwart a hacker or terrorist's malicious intentions. More than forty network providers that make up the backbone of the Internet have agreements to help distribute each other's Internet traffic in the event of a disaster. These companies are trying to improve their ability to reroute and reconnect data flow should a major provider be forced offline by a cyberattack.

Despite all the doomsaying and spinning of nightmare scenarios about cyberterrorism by government and intelligence agencies, antivirus software manufacturers, cybersecurity consultants, and Internet conspiracy theorists, the actual threat of a devastating and crippling attack, while real, is not nearly as high as we are often led to believe. The fact of the matter is that actual reported instances of cyber infiltration have not been caused by terrorists, but rather ordinary criminals or "joyriding" hackers trying to cause mischief or access "free" resources. Yet our vigilance and wariness are still valuable. This heightened sense of danger and alertness may keep our worst fears from becoming a reality. It may even be the force that foils any cyberterrorist who hopes to destroy our computer-driven infrastructure and slow modern technological society to a predigital crawl.

Glossary

blasphemous Grossly disrespectful toward what is believed to be sacred.

breach To get past something's defenses.

cybercrime The use of a computer to commit fraud, distribute obscene or offensive content, or engage in harassment.

cyberwarfare The use of computers and the Internet to conduct hostile acts, usually between two states.

detection The act of discovering something, such as a crime, a breach, or an error.

encryption The act of converting data into code for security purposes.

exploit To use or manipulate to one's own advantage.

firewall Part of a computer system or network designed to block unauthorized access.

flaw A defect or weakness in someone or something.

generator A machine that converts one form of energy into another; a machine that can generate electricity when the usual electrical system goes down.

hacktivism The use of computers to achieve social or political goals.

infrastructure The basic physical and organizational structures needed for the operation of a society or enterprise, or the services and facilities necessary for an economy to function. The term typically refers to the technical structures that support a society, such as roads, water supply, sewers, power grids, telecommunications, etc.

intrusion The act of entering another's property without right or permission.

malicious Full of vicious or mischievous motivation or intent.
manifesto A public declaration of one's intentions and/or ideas.
monitoring The act of observing something and keeping a record of the observations.
obscene Offensive to good taste.
perpetrator Someone who does something illegal; someone who commits a crime.
pharmaceutical Relating to the drugs used in medical treatment.
phishing Fraudulent e-mails that look like legitimate correspondence from reputable businesses that seek to persuade you to provide sensitive personal information, such as credit card numbers, Social Security numbers, user names, and passwords.
prankster Someone who plays practical jokes on others.
scenario An imagined sequence of events.
subversive Someone who is radically opposed to the government or society and the way things are done.
Trojan horse Malicious software that looks like legitimate software but, once installed on a computer, can delete files and destroy information.
unspecified Not stated precisely or in detail.
virus A malicious program that arrives in file attachments and damages a computer's hardware, software, and files.
vulnerable Open to being attacked or hurt.
worm A malicious program that replicates itself and travels from computer to computer by, for example, sending itself to everyone in someone's e-mail address book.

For More Information

Canadian Cyber Incident Response Centre
Public Safety Canada
269 Laurier Avenue West
Ottawa, ON K1A 0P8
Canada
(800) 830-3118
Web site: http://www.publicsafety.gc.ca/prg/em/ccirc/index-eng.aspx

The Canadian Cyber Incident Response Centre is an organization that is responsible for monitoring threats and coordinating a national response to any cybersecurity incident in Canada.

Federal Bureau of Investigation (FBI)
Edgar Hoover Building
935 Pennsylvania Avenue NW
Washington, DC 20535-0001
(202) 324-3000
Web site: http://www.fbi.gov/cyberinvest/cyberhome.htm

The FBI's Web site offers an inside look at the government agency's cyber operations, which try to stop the most serious of cyber intrusions and the spreading of malicious code.

National Institute of Standards and Technology (NIST)
100 Bureau Drive, Stop 1070
Gaithersburg, MD 20899-1070
(301) 975-NIST (6478)
Web site: http://www.nist.gov/index.html

The NIST is a nonregulatory federal agency within the U.S. Department of Commerce. Its mission is to advance technology to enhance economic security and improve our quality of life.

Oak Ridge National Laboratory
P.O. Box 2008
Oak Ridge, TN 37831-6252
(865) 574-8162
Web site: http://www.ornl.gov/tac
The Technology Advantage Center at Oak Ridge National Laboratory is involved in the research and development of technologies to help in homeland security and national defense.

UC-Davis Computer Security Lab
Department of Computer Science
University of California, Davis
One Shields Avenue
Davis, CA 95616-8562
Web site: http://seclab.cs.ucdavis.edu
The Computer Security Lab's mission is to improve the current state of computer security through research and teaching.

U.S. Department of Justice
Criminal Division (Computer Crime and Intellectual Property Section)
John C. Keeney Building, Suite 600
10th & Constitution Avenue NW
Washington, DC 20530

(202) 514-2000
Web site: http://www.cybercrime.gov
The Computer Crime and Intellectual Property Section of the U.S. Department of Justice maintains a database of reported Internet breaches.

Web Sites

Due to the changing nature of Internet links, Rosen Publishing has developed an online list of Web sites related to the subject of this book. This site is updated regularly. Please use this link to access the list:

http://www.rosenlinks.com/doom/cybe

For Further Reading

Ananda, Mitra. *Digital Security: Cyber Terror and Cyber Security* (The Digital World). New York, NY: Chelsea House Publishers, 2009.

Appleman, Dan. *Always Use Protection: A Teen's Guide to Safe Computing*. Berkeley, CA: Apress, 2004.

Bailey, Diane. *Cyber Ethics* (Cyber Citizenship and Cyber Safety). New York, NY: Rosen Central, 2008.

Combs, Cindy C., and Martin W. Slann. *Encyclopedia of Terrorism* (Facts On File Library of World History). New York, NY: Facts On File, 2007.

Day-MacLeod, Deirdre. *Viruses and Spam* (Cyber Citizenship and Cyber Safety). New York, NY: Rosen Central, 2008.

Haugen, Hayley Mitchell, and Susan Musser, eds. *Internet Safety* (Issues That Concern You). Farmington Hills, MI: Greenhaven Press, 2008.

Levin, John, and Jack Levin. *Domestic Terrorism* (Roots of Terrorism). New York, NY: Chelsea House Publishers, 2006.

Newman, Matthew. *You Have Mail: True Stories of Cybercrime* (24/7: Science Behind the Scenes). New York, NY: Scholastic, 2007.

Orr, Tamra. *Privacy and Hacking* (Cyber Citizenship and Cyber Safety). New York, NY: Rosen Central, 2008.

Platt, Richard, and John Townsend. *Cyber Crime*. Mankato, MN: Raintree, 2005.

Bibliography

Bannerman, Lucy. "Genius Who Wasted $1bn? My Son Gary McKinnon Was Just Looking for ET." TimesOnline (UK). January 13, 2009. Retrieved April 2009 (http://www.timesonline.co.uk/tol/news/uk/crime/article5505489.ece).

BBC News. "Obama Begins Technology Security Review." February 10, 2009. Retrieved February 2009 (http://news.bbc.co.uk/2/hi/technology/7880695.stm).

Bridis, Ted. "Senior White House Advisor on Cyber Security Confirms Resignation." Channelweb, January 31, 2003. Retrieved December 2008 (http://www.crn.com/security/18822494;jsessionid=0BCZWZA4F1MI4QSNDLPCKH0CJUNN2JVN).

Cauley, Leslie. "NSA Has Massive Database of Americans' Phone Calls." *USA Today*, May 11, 2006. Retrieved March 2009 (http://www.usatoday.com/news/washington/2006-05-10-nsa_x.htm).

Computer Weekly. "'Major' Virus Incident at Barts and the London." ComputerWeekly.com, November 19, 2008. Retrieved April 2009 (http://www.computerweekly.com/blogs/tony_collins/2008/11/major-virus-incident-at-barts.html).

Dacey, Robert F. *Critical Infrastructure Protection Challenges and Efforts to Secure Control Systems: Report to Congressional Requesters*. U.S. General Accounting Office. Darby, PA: Diane Publishing, 2004.

Denning, Dorothy. "Is Cyber Terror Next?" SSRC.org, November 1, 2001. Retrieved April 2009 (http://essays.ssrc.org/sept11/essays/denning.htm).

Elias, Marilyn. "Most Teen Hackers More Curious Than Criminal." *USA Today*, August 19, 2007. Retrieved March

2009 (http://www.usatoday.com/news/health/2007-08-19-teen-hackers_N.htm).

Independent Online. "U.S. 'Not Prepared' for Cyberterrorism." December 4, 2003. Retrieved December 2008 (http://www.iol.co.za/index.php?click_id=31&art_id=qw1070507887505S323&set_id=1).

Institute for Security Technology Studies. "Examining the Cyber Capabilities of Islamic Terrorist Groups." Dartmouth College, 2003. Retrieved March 2009 (http://www.ists.dartmouth.edu/library/164.pdf).

Jackson, William. "Oak Ridge Explores Cybots," *Government Computer News*, February 19, 2009. Retrieved April 2009 (http://www.gcn.com/Articles/2009/02/23/Oak-Ridge-explores-cybots.aspx).

James, Michael S. "Cyber Attack Possible During Time of Terror." ABC News, September 23, 2003. Retrieved January 2009 (http://abcnews.go.com/Technology/story?id=97157).

Kessler, Ronald. *The Terrorist Watch: Inside the Desperate Race to Stop the Next Attack*. New York, NY: Crown Forum, 2007.

McCullough, Declan. "The Sentinel." *Wired*, March 2002.

Miller, Joshua Rhett. "Colonies of 'Cybots' May Defend Government Network." *FOX News*, March 6, 2009. Retrieved March 2009 (http://www.foxnews.com/story/0,2933,505159,00.html).

Mitnick, Kevin D. *The Art of Deception*. New York, NY: Wiley Publishing, Inc., 2002.

National Defense. "Net Defense: Big-Bucks Cyber Security Program Proposed." April 2008. Retrieved February 2009 (http://findarticles.com/p/articles/mi_hb6540/is_200804/ai_n25909474?tag=content;col1).

National Institute of Standards and Technology. "Comprehensive National Cyber Security Initiative: Leap-Ahead Security Technologies." NIST.gov, February 1, 2008. Retrieved January 2009 (http://www.nist.gov/public_affairs/factsheet/cyber2009.html).

Poulson, Kevin. "Did Hackers Cause the 2003 Northeast Blackout? Umm, No." *Wired*, May 29, 2008. Retrieved March 2009 (http://blog.wired.com/27bstroke6/2008/05/did-hackers-cau.html).

Robertson, Jordan. "Conficker Worm Set to Spring to Life." Associated Press, March 31, 2009. Retrieved March 2009 (http://news.aol.com/article/conficker-worm-virus-april-1/402022?icid=main|main|dl1|link3|http%3A%2F%2Fnews.aol.com%2Farticle%2Fconficker-worm-virus-april-1%2F402022).

Standage, Tom. "The Mouse That Might Roar." CFO.com, November 1, 2002. Retrieved April 2009 (http://www.cfo.com/article.cfm/3007058/c_2984283/?f=archives).

Verton, Dan. *Black Ice*. New York, NY: McGraw-Hill Professional, 2003.

White, Jonathan R. *Terrorism: An Introduction*. Stamford, CT: Wadsworth Thomson Learning, 2002.

Index

About the Author

Jacqueline Ching has written for *Newsweek* and the *Seattle Times*. She has written several books on matters relating to public policy, government, public and private security, and pressing social concerns and civic issues.

Photo Credits

Cover, pp. 1, 14, 16, 26, 38, 46–47, 49 © AP Photos; pp. 4–5 © Robert Giroux/Getty Images; p. 8 © Greg Finley/Getty Images; pp. 21, 40 © Newscom; p. 23 © 20th Century Fox/Everett Collection; p. 28 © Mason Morfit/Getty Images; p. 31 © Adri Berger/Getty Images; p. 33 © Greg Pease/Getty Images; pp. 50–51 © Fredrik Skold/Getty Images.

Designer: Sam Zavieh; Photo Researcher: Marty Levick